PORNOGRAPHY AND FEMINISM

The Case Against Censorship

by
Feminists Against Censorship

Edited by
Gillian Rodgerson & Elizabeth
Wilson

LAWRENCE & WISHART
LONDON

Lawrence & Wishart Ltd
144a Old South Lambeth Road
London SW8 1XX

This edition first published in 1991

Text design by Jan Brown
Photoset in North Wales by
Derek Doyle & Associates, Mold, Clwyd
Printed and bound in Great Britain by
Dotesios, Trowbridge

Contents

Acknowledgements

Pornography and Feminism was written by members of the Feminists Against Censorship Publications Group: Alison Assiter, Avedon Carol, Mary McIntosh, Nettie Pollard, Gillian Rodgerson and Elizabeth Wilson. We would like to give special thanks to Sue O'Sullivan. Thanks also to Mandy Merck for information on changes in obscenity law.

1. Introduction

In recent years, the issue of pornography has engendered an intense debate in the feminist community. Dismissed by some as diversionary, it is a debate whose stakes, we feel, are high. Will feminism, having achieved some gains, capitulate to conservative forces, or will it continue to take a stand for the liberation of women in all domains, including the difficult and contradictory domain of sexual expression? We are still asking in the mid- eighties what *do* women want, and the answer is that women have multiple desires and goals. We want to be valued equally with men as earners, but we don't want to contribute to the pollution of the planet and the exploitation of other human beings. We want to be safe from attack and abuse, in our private lives as well as in the public sphere, but we don't want that safety at the cost of challenge, risk, exploration and pleasure. Safety and adventure represent conflicting demands: the relationship between the two, and how to negotiate it, is a key issue in the current debate.

Caught Looking: Feminism, Pornography and Censorship
(Caught Looking Inc (eds) The Real Comet Press,
Seattle 1986)

What divided the American feminist community in the mid-eighties divides us in Britain today.

Attempts are being made, in the name of feminism, to whip up public feeling against pornography and add to the laws that restrict its production and distribution. The other sides of feminism are in danger of being submerged. The exploration of sexual possibilities, which has been at times painful but at times immensely liberating, is condemned as a luxury that we are too embattled to afford. The grand project of changing basic structures of power gives way to the short-sighted expedient of clapping handcuffs on what anti-pornography feminists regard as the most excessive manifestations of male power. The long efforts to understand the complexities of patriarchal culture and then to challenge and change it, get short-circuited by an approach that simply takes up one side of a polarized argument within and outside feminism – a side which has allies among reactionary forces, and which has lost sight of the wider aims of feminism.

In the United States the battle lines were drawn up between the supporters of the Minneapolis Ordinance and the Feminist Anti-Censorship Taskforce (FACT). In 1984 Minneapolis City Council in Minnesota passed an ordinance, drafted by feminists Andrea Dworkin and Catherine MacKinnon, which would allow women to take civil action against anyone involved in the production, distribution or sale of pornography on the grounds that they had been harmed by the image of women that it portrayed; it was vetoed by the mayor. Backed by anti-feminist conservatives, a revised version was passed by the Indianapolis City Council in Indiana and attempts were made to introduce similar legislation in other places including Los Angeles, California and Cambridge, Massachusetts, in the following year. FACT, working with other feminists and media groups, co-ordinated opposition in various cities and a two-year legal battle ended in the Supreme Court declaring the Indianapolis ordinance unconstitutional.

Alongside this legislative battle went a struggle for the hearts and minds of the women's movement. On the one side were those who see not just sexual violence but sexual intercourse in general as the key moment in women's oppression. They organized emotionally charged meetings and barnstorming lecture tours in which the most extreme violent images were shown as representative of pornography (Andrea Dworkin said: 'The eroticization of murder is the essence of pornography.') and in which women who had been sexually abused in various ways gave testimony to the horror they had experienced and claimed it was caused by pornography. For them it was essential to put pornography centre-stage as 'a practice that is central to the subordination of women' (MacKinnon in the Minneapolis hearings), because they needed to argue that it violated women's civil rights in a serious way in order to justify limiting freedom of speech.

On the other side were those who recognize the oppressive nature of dominant heterosexual culture and practices but who, for a variety of reasons, oppose legal restrictions on pornography. There was the civil liberties argument, which was able to appeal to a vigorous tradition in American thought and to invoke the First Amendment to the American Constitution – which guarantees freedom of speech – to reject restrictions, even when they are couched in terms of the right to sue for damages in a civil court.

The crucial difference was, however, that there was a different analysis of women's oppression which saw sexuality and violence as only a part of a larger system of inequality and saw contradictions within sexuality from women's point of view. The main contradiction was summed up in a book title: *Pleasure and Danger* (Carole Vance (ed) Routledge 1985). Anti-censorship feminists insisted that the way to counter the dangers associated with sex was not to censor images of women as sexual objects but to challenge the central assumptions about sexuality which determine sexual ideology in our culture. It was important not to close down on sex and narrow the boundaries of the permissible but to expand the possibilities of women's sexual pleasure. After all, part of feminism had been a flowering of books, magazines and films on feminist erotic themes, encouraging women to be sexually expressive, not repressive. It was also necessary to consider the many other factors which create danger for women in sexual and other relationships.

In Britain the debates have taken longer to develop but have followed a similar course, although here there is relatively little space for local legislation; nor, of course, do we have the same constitutional right to freedom of expression as exists in the United States. In the late 1980s two feminist-led organizations were set up in Britain to combat pornography. The Campaign Against Pornography and Censorship concentrated its efforts on obtaining legislation similar to the MacKinnon/Dworkin ordinance in the United States. The Campaign Against Pornography preferred to use more high-profile direct action; its 'Off the Shelf' campaign of local protests against newsagents and bookshops that stocked 'soft core' porn magazines gained the support of the National Union of Students and several thousand signatures on a petition.

So far the magazines remain in the shops but the campaigns against pornography have attracted support from the mainstream political parties. We would have expected the traditionalist wing of the Conservative Party and MPs with strong religious affiliations to support any drive against pornography. After twelve years of right-wing Toryism, the moral right is riding high and has a close involvement with feminist attempts at legislation; Jill Knight MP, for example, is among its supporters. What is more surprising is the zeal with which the Labour Party has taken up the issue. Although, as we shall show later on, the theory about sexuality and male behaviour upon which these campaigns ultimately rests comes from 'cultural' or 'radical' feminism which has always seen men as the 'main enemy', many socialists have felt that pornography was an aspect of capitalist pollution and profiteering. At a time when left-wing politics is comprehensively marginalized, the anti-porn campaign can seem like an issue that can be supported on feminist and anti-exploitative grounds. It also appeals to the moralistic and religious strand within the Labour Party (the 'Methodist legacy') and to the more authoritarian aspects of the Fabian tradition. So the Labour Party has cloaked its attempts at censorship in a mantle of feminist respectability. More cynically, it may seem like a vote-catcher with no 'loony left' tag and one that will further the desired image of a thoroughly respectable Labour Party.

Ranged against the pro-censorship feminists is our group: Feminists Against Censorship. We founded the group in order to counter the increasing dominance of the censorship lobby and to ensure that an alternative feminist view is heard. One of our successes so far has been to convince the National Council for Civil Liberties (Liberty) to abandon its short-lived support for draft legislation that would place comprehensive restrictions on the availability of sexually explicit material. Later in this pamphlet we will discuss the bill, sponsored by Labour MP Dawn Primarolo, which would also restrict the availability of such material. All in all, it seems quite likely that legislation will succeed in spite of the civil liberties argument.

As feminists we have a responsibility to be critical of those images we find sexist, racist or exploitative and to counter them in the most effective way there is, not by seeking to get them banned, but by initiating a much more wide-ranging debate about sex, by lobbying for better sex education in schools, by creating more informed, tolerant and responsible social attitudes to the expression of sexuality, and by supporting those who are creating an alternative body of sexual images for women. As we said in our first leaflet, issued in 1989:

> Women need open and safe communication about sexual matters, including the power relations of sex. We don't need new forms of guilt parading under the banner of political correctness. We need a safe, legal working environment for sex workers, not repressive laws or an atmosphere of social stigma that empowers police and punters to brutalize them. We need sexually explicit material produced by and for women, freed from the control of right wingers and misogynists, whether they sit on the board of directors or the board of censors. We need an analysis of violence that empowers women and protects them at the same time. We need a feminism willing to tackle issues of class and race and to deal with the variety of oppressions in the world, not to reduce all oppressions to pornography.

In *Pornography and Feminism: The Case Against Censorship*, we look at some of the complexities and contradictions of pornography from a feminist point of view which has led us to the belief that pornography is not a straightforward evil and that increasing legal controls are not the answer.

2. Pornography and Censorship: Siamese Twins?

Pornography as a term, and as a fact of life, is relatively recent in Western history. It would not be a great over-simplification to say that it developed along with certain aspects of middle-class morality in the nineteenth century. As this morality of prudery and sexual restraint displaced both aristocratic licentiousness and the rules-of thumb of earlier Christian teaching and rural custom, so a separate space, outside the walls of the new respectability, was created for everything that prudery condemned. It was very typical of the Victorian period to create a deep chasm between respectable and unrespectable, and the opposed yet twin images of the Madonna and Magdalene were often used to divide women in these terms. In the cities prostitution flourished as never before but was also more sternly punished and stigmatized. Bourgeois morality projected onto prostitutes, and onto the working classes and 'savages', many of the desires that it sought to suppress. So it is perhaps not surprising that the term 'pornography' literally means 'pictures or writing about prostitutes'.

PORNOGRAPHY AND CENSORSHIP

Originally this word was a rare and rather scholarly one – derived from a single instance in classical Greek writing – used for works on social policy and public administration for the regulation of prostitutes. In 1769, Restif de la Bretonne was able to publish a book on this subject called *The Pornographer* and the Oxford English Dictionary continues to give this as the primary meaning to this day:

1. A description of prostitutes or of prostitution, as a matter of public hygiene.
2. Description of the life, manners, etc. of prostitutes and their patrons; hence, the expression or suggestion of obscene or unchaste subjects in literature or art.

As Walter Kendrick has pointed out in his book, *The Secret Museum* (Viking 1987), 'a large step is taken in that "hence" ', for it is a link that has only come to seem obvious as a result of the curiously obsessive repression of sexuality of the nineteenth century. In the eighteenth century Restif could write on prostitution in a rather lighthearted way. By the nineteenth century works on social hygiene and prostitution had to be at great pains to be scientific and to avoid any suggestion of the salacious. Yet such works proliferated in Britain and France and it is hard to believe that their sales were not helped by an avid but forbidden interest in all things sexual.

According to Walter Kendrick, the term pornography first began to bridge this gap in the mid-nineteenth century when scholars were called upon to catalogue and display the pictures and artefacts unearthed in the excavation of the Roman city of Pompeii. Vases and walls throughout the town were decorated with paintings of sexual pursuit and intercourse and there were erect stone phalluses in domestic courtyards and at many street corners. Victorians found it hard to reconcile such widespread lasciviousness with a great civilization, and the museum-keepers chose to identify the rooms painted with sexual scenes as brothels. All the items that were thought too obscene to be displayed in public were conserved in a separate collection in the National Museum of Naples: the 'secret museum'. In 1866 the first systematic catalogue of this locked room was entitled the 'pornographic collection'.

The people excluded from the locked room were women, children and the uneducated. When an illustrated catalogue was printed in 1877, it was in an expensive edition which only the wealthy could afford; the genitals were miniaturized or blurred and the text was larded with erudite Latin and Greek quotations. In this way pornography was born as a genre available to bourgeois men who could declare that their interest was scholarly. What defined it from the start was that it was forbidden to the general public.

During the course of the nineteenth and early twentieth centuries, the definition of pornography developed and changed with shifts in the boundaries of what should be available in public and particularly what should be available to the most 'vulnerable and corruptible' members of society. In England and Wales this boundary was succinctly defined in 1868 when Lord Justice Cockburn formulated the test of obscenity to be applied to the 1857 Obscene Publications Act:

> A tendency ... to deprave and corrupt those whose minds are open to such immoral influences, and into whose hands a publication of this sort may fall.

Ironically or not, the test was first formulated in a judgement against a Protestant Political Union political tract, in which the prurient questions Catholic priests were supposed to have asked women in confessional were exposed. From the start, then, pornography and censorship were an inseparable couple and censorship was part of a particularly paternalistic form of patriarchal domination that had its heyday in the Victorian era.

During the twentieth century, criteria of scientific and literary merit were established which could outweigh 'obscenity' and the courts were required to take into account the work as a whole, rather than to select out particular passages.

> For the purposes of this Act an article shall be deemed obscene if its effect ... is, if taken as a whole, such as to deprave and corrupt persons who are likely, in all the circumstances, to read, see or hear the matter contained or embodied in it ... [The defendant shall

not be convicted] ... if publication of the article in question is justified as being for the public good ... in the interests of science, literature, art or learning, or of other objects of general concern.

Subsequent appeal rulings have further established that shock or disgust by itself does not indicate obscenity, since works which provoke such feelings might actually *discourage* depravity.

The general line of development from the mid-nineteenth century to the present day is that the obscene becomes identified with a particular genre – pornography – usually meaning writing or pictures (and later films and videos) produced with the purpose of sexual arousal and having no 'redeeming' value. The assumption is that to set out intentionally to produce sexual arousal is despicable, but if the main objective of the work is artistic or scientific and the possibility of sexual arousal is only incidental, then these 'higher' purposes may justify publication. The courts thus undertook to make aesthetic judgements, apparently unaware that class prejudice and aesthetics go hand in hand. The 'educated man', and nowadays, indeed, the 'educated woman', can have erotic images packaged with arts and sciences. The 'uneducated' should either do without or make do with the popular press where it comes wrapped up with 'news'.

The Obscene Publications Act is still the main law on pornography, though alongside it there is a welter of complicated and overlapping statutes and common-law offences relating to indecent displays, child pornography, film censorship, the sale of goods and importing indecent materials. Yet despite all these laws, during this century illicit pornography – 'dirty' postcards, books and magazines from abroad, blue movies – has proliferated.

The late 1950s and the 1960s are often referred to as a period of permissive reforms: the ending of the death penalty and of suicide as a crime, the liberalization of laws on drinking, gambling, homosexuality, contraception, abortion, divorce, theatre censorship and Sunday entertainments. But the story in relation to pornography is not one of increasing permissiveness. The 1959 Obscene Publications Act, it is true, exempted 'serious literature', but at the same time it strengthened the law by widening the powers of the police and making it easier for them to seize material. The 1964 Obscene Publications Act further tightened the law by closing various loopholes about evidence and extending it to cover photographic negatives as well as material for sale. This last point is interesting, because it was the first time that the law recognized, and sought to regulate, the production as well as the distribution of pornography. It was a recognition that obscenity was no longer just a category of harmful materials but an increasingly separate branch of publishing with its own technology, entrepreneurs and outlets.

The Williams Committee on Obscenity and Film Censorship attempted to introduce some order into an increasingly chaotic situation. Its report, published in

1979, supported the liberal principle that the main concern of the law should be with identifiable harms. In this it followed the view of the Wolfenden Committee of 1957, which considered that the function of the law was not to enforce morality but 'to preserve public order and decency, to protect the citizen from what is offensive or injurious, and to provide sufficient safeguards against exploitation and corruption of others, particularly those who are especially vulnerable.'

The report surveyed the data on international comparisons of sexual crime rates and the availability of pornographic materials as well as the evidence of social psychologists, which at that time appeared contradictory. Finally, it rejected the argument that pornography acts as a stimulus to sexual violence. The report recognized that the production of pornography might involve risks of physical injury, or the participation of those below the age of consent, which would need to be dealt with by the existing relevant criminal laws. However, it rejected the 'deprave and corrupt' test as too vague and the 'public good' defence as too reliant on aesthetic consensus and expert opinion. These concepts were of no help in relation to 'indifferent' works. Instead, the harm identified was the possible offensiveness of some materials to many people. In order to guarantee individual rights and at the same time prevent this harm, it recommended that items whose 'unrestricted sale would give, in the estimate of a magistrate, offence to a reasonable person' should be confined to special shops, with blank windows and posted warnings, for those aged eighteen or over. The same solution was applied successfully when the betting laws were liberalized in 1960, and similar solutions have often been proposed for prostitution.

With the election of the Conservative government of Margaret Thatcher in 1979, the Williams Committee's recommendations were set aside in favour of increasing restrictions of representations through piecemeal legislation. In 1981 the Indecent Displays (Control) Act prohibited the public display of indecent material. In 1982 the Local Government (Miscellaneous Provisions) Act gave local authorities the power to licence 'sex establishments'. This Act also offered, for the first time, a definition of the specifically cinematic material to be controlled as that which portrays or is intended to stimulate 'sexual activity' or 'acts of force or restraint which are associated with sexual activity' or that which portrays 'genital organs or urinary or excretory functions'.

This approach to definition in legislation is sometimes called the 'laundry list'. It is usually disparaged by lawyers in England and Wales on the grounds that there are often cases which fall within the spirit of the law but have not been included in the list, leaving little room for judicial interpretation. In response to the 'video nasties' scare over the distribution of violent horror features on cassette in the early 1980s, the 1984 Video Recordings Act used the same laundry list approach with a vengeance. Instead of a general stipulation against moral harm, such as that in the Obscene Publications Act, particular images – of genitalia, excretory functions, acts of sex or gross violence, or anything which might 'stimulate or encourage' such acts – were specified in a list of representations requiring classification prior to distribution. Previously the power to permit a film to be shown or not rested with local authorities, who took the advice of the British Board of Film Classification (BBFC) but interpreted it to suit their own area; London, for instance, being notably more liberal. Now the Board became national censors, legally empowered to deny certificates altogether or to grant them subject to certain cuts being made. By November 16 1987, BBFC director James Ferman could declare to *The Independent* that, 'the notorious "video nasties" have largely disappeared from the shops because the Board has refused to grant them certificates.'

Alongside this rag-bag of laws enforced by the police, there are the powers of HM Customs and Excise to search for and seize any 'indecent' articles imported into this country. 'Indecency' is a much broader and more vague category than 'obscenity' and, because the defence of 'public good' does not apply here, sex education and safer sex materials can be seized under Customs legislation. The onus is on the importer to challenge the Customs officers' decision and to satisfy a magistrates' court that the article is not obscene. In 1985 it was the Customs and Excise rather than the police who mounted 'Operation Tiger' against the London bookshop Gay's The Word. They brought a total of 100 criminal charges against the eight directors of the shop and seized copies of 142 imported titles, including works by Jean Genet, Allen Ginsburg, Edmund White, Tennessee Williams, Kate Millett, Oscar Wilde and Jean Paul Sartre. A year later all charges were dropped, partly because it became clear that British law is out of step with European Community law on this matter. But the British law remains on the statute book and its tougher approach to imported material reflects the demonizing of the alien; the notion that 'we pure British' need to be protected against 'tides of foreign filth'.

Meanwhile, 'soft core' pornography, mainly in magazine stories and photographs, is openly on sale. It has become highly standardized with a limited repertoire of recognizable plots and poses. At first sight this soft core pornography may appear to be free from social control because it is the type of material that *is* permitted. But in fact it is very much a product of social control. Its range and explicitness are completely determined by what the distributors consider will be sufficiently 'hot' and risqué to sell well, but sufficiently 'acceptable' in law to be displayed in public.

It is clear, then, from a glance at the history of pornography that, until feminism entered the debate, pornography and censoriousness were an inseparable couple. All our definitions of pornography depended upon this; an essential ingredient of pornography was the desire to shock, to cross the boundaries, to explore forbidden zones. Repressive sexual morality always tends to foster and feed its own 'worst enemies' in this way.

Into this traditional ritual of laws and law-breakers, feminism has tried to intrude with completely new considerations. Feminism has wanted to side-step the question of the boundaries of sexual decency and focus on the fact that most pornography is produced for heterosexual men, that it consists of masculine sexual fantasies, mainly about women. Some feminist writers have gone so far as to claim that pornography lies at the very heart of women's oppression, either because, as Robin Morgan put it 'pornography is the theory – rape is the practice' of male domination or because 'pornography *is* violence against women,' as Andrea Dworkin says. Such writers have tended to paint a very lurid picture of pornography, as if it were all images of rape, sadism and degradation in which women are the victims.

Anyone can see that much pornography represents a sexuality in which women are passive and men active, and women are desired and men desire. Pornography does contain stereotypes of women which feminism wishes to challenge. In this respect it is similar to many other genres, from Renaissance painting to *Vogue* magazine, which have been subjected to feminist critiques. This is not to say that pornography is good, simply that most of it is no worse than a great deal of the rest of the patriarchal and misogynist culture which it reflects.

If pornography is defined, as the Williams Committee defined it, as representations that are both sexually explicit and have as their function the sexual arousal of their audience, then it is not *necessarily* oppressive to women. Indeed, many feminists have wanted to challenge the old taboos about sexual material, to talk more frankly about women's bodies – and men's – and to explore what we find arousing. It is certainly possible to imagine a pornography *for* women, though no one could guarantee that it would never be used by men in a misogynist way.

Those feminists who recently have been arguing in favour of censorship have done so on the basis of a new definition of pornography which identifies it with sexually explicit images of degradation and violence against women. This was the approach used in the Minneapolis Ordinance in the United States and it was adopted in 1990 by Dawn Pimarolo MP, for her Location of Pornographic Materials Bill. Clause 3 of this bill reads:

3(1) Pornographic material means film and video and any printed matter which, for the purposes of sexual arousal or titillation, depicts women, or parts of women's bodies, as objects, things or commodities, or in sexually humiliating or degrading poses or being subjected to violence.

3(2) The reference to women in sub-section (1) above includes men.

The justification for such formulations is the belief that sexually arousing images have a special efficacy in producing violence against women. (Sub-section 3(2) was added only from a concern, misguided in this context, for gender equality.) As we shall show later, there is no evidence for this belief. Is there an unacknowledged reason why these campaigners have focused on *sexually* degrading images and ignored the myriad forms of non-sexual degradation? Is the underlying reason that they themselves feel revulsion at the more sexually explicit images, or is it that they believe that a campaign against pornography can gain wider support in a way that no other recent feminist cause has done? The problem is that many women feel very ambivalent about pornography, welcoming images we find erotic but being quite disturbed by others. In a society where sex is so freighted with implications of non-conformity and disorder, it is difficult for women to express our pro-sex feelings in public. It is much easier to express the other side of the ambivalence: the disapproval. This has traditional respectability on its side and so is more likely to find a public voice and public support. Pornography is an area where there will be widespread support for further control but for reasons that are very foreign to feminism.

The pro-censorship, anti-pornography feminists are

plugging into a pre-feminist debate although they claim to have gone beyond it. They are against *degrading* images of women, or images they consider to be degrading. But their allies are against *sexually explicit* images of any kind and against any material that aims to be sexually arousing. As Feminists Against Censorship we wish to challenge and to question this equation of the sexually arousing with the degrading. Otherwise the alliance of the anti-pornography feminists with the traditional moralists may succeed in reversing many of the gains that have been made during the twentieth century.

3. Feminism and Sexual Violence

Feminists have always campaigned against male violence. In the nineteenth century, for example, feminist outrage at what they called 'wife torture' was widespread and, among other things, feminists succeeded in bringing about a change in the law in Britain so that women subjected to abuse might be able to obtain a legal separation from violent husbands. In the quiescent years of feminism there was less concern, although in the 1930s Virginia Woolf railed against masculinity in its militarist guise. But since the 1960s feminists have once again made the struggle against the violence of men towards women (and children) a major priority.

In a caricature of feminist positions, it is sometimes suggested that only 'cultural' or 'radical' feminists have opposed male violence, while 'socialist' feminists have been exclusively concerned with issues related to work and welfare. This is not true and these labels do an injustice to all feminists. Radical or cultural feminists have usually been very critical of the injustices found in capitalist societies. The great majority of socialist feminists have been aware that 'socialism' will not automatically eradicate violence and aggression, and that there is more to women's oppression than economic exploitation. They have known for many years that Eastern European socialism was deeply flawed; one reason for this was the failure of those societies to recognize women's continuing oppression. Instead, the governments of the Soviet bloc insisted that a command economy had somehow wiped out the many complex problems of gender relations, multiple inequalities and human aggression.

For the past twenty years feminists have campaigned to increase public awareness of the way in which men wield power over women in many different ways and to redress this imbalance. One important focus of criticism has been the way in which western popular culture represents women. Feminists have always objected to sexist media imagery. One of the feminist objections to page three models, to advertising in general and to other representations of women in the mass media, was that they were over sexualized. Young women were normally presented as highly desirable in a conventional way: slim, blonde (white, in fact), or, if not, then they were ugly figures of fun or condemnation: witches, mothers-in-law, spinsters, lesbians.

Feminists pointed out that advertising and fashion spreads borrowed some of their poses from magazines such as *Penthouse* and *Mayfair*. These images were objectionable not because they were sexual, but because women were granted approval *only* to the extent that they were perceived as sexually desirable and sexually available as defined by prevailing male norms. However, representations which positioned women exclusively as mothers were attacked in equal measure. Feminists wanted a much wider recognition of women as capable, strong and independent, and wanted women to be portrayed as such.

The solution, however, was never seen in terms of censorship or the paternalistic protection of women by the state. It was recognized that the only lasting road to women's liberation was a general strengthening of the position of women in society. Economic independence, together with the right to motherhood without financial dependency on men or the state (i.e. the right to maternity leave, job security and other rights), were seen as central; women would never control their own bodies until they became less financially dependent upon men. If there was one central plank of women's subordination, it was the unequal contract between the sexes whereby women exchanged sexual services and domestic labour in return for economic support. In other words, feminists attempted to de-link sexual relationships (marriage or cohabitation) on the one hand from economic dependence on the other. Women's oppression was held in place by an interlocking system of related oppressions: economic exploitation at work, injustice in the welfare system, male supremacy in the family and oppressive sexual ideologies. For that reason, the infamous 'cohabitation rule' of the social security system (the ruling that a woman living with a man is considered to be financially dependent on him) and the refusal to allow cohabiting adults to claim benefit independently, were denounced as key expressions of women's subordination.

Feminists campaigned to bring women greater independence in many different ways. Women's Aid set up a network of refuges for battered women and, with the help of Jo Richardson, got the law changed so that, in theory at least, it became easier for women to obtain legal redress against a violent partner. Rape crisis centres were set up and legal and police attitudes to women who had been raped were challenged.

These campaigns were multi-faceted. They offered women basic practical help: a roof over their heads, legal assistance, help with the day to day problems of benefits and child custody and the vital, confidence-building supports of feminist counselling, self-defence and collective solidarity. In the late 1970s and early 1980s feminist trade unionists campaigned around the issue of sexual harrassment at work; there were repeated calls for better street lighting and better public transport on which women, to a far greater extent than men, have to rely.

Campaigns went hand in hand with feminist attempts to develop theories to explain why it was that so many men perpetrated crimes of violence, whether sexual or not, against women. Some feminists saw violence as inherently male ('all men are rapists'), and this belief was consistent with one particular theory of human behaviour: 'biologism', the view that human beings are determined and programmed by their biology (as other species are, to a greater or lesser extent). A section of the women's movement has promoted the view that, just as women are 'naturally' nurturant, peace-loving and so on, so men are doomed by nature to be violent, dominant and aggressive. This is, of course, an extremely conservative view, the only difference being that feminists tend to denounce 'male' characteristics, while arguing that 'women's' characteristics should be more highly valued. Feminists who campaign against pornography often deny that they hold biologistic views, yet their positioning of men as necessarily violent and of women as always passive and victimized, closely follows this conservative stereotype. Such an approach tends to see all women as the same and all men as the same. It takes no account of class or ethnic differences, for example. According to this view, all men are predators and all women victims.

Yet curiously, this deterministic theory was combined with another, that of behaviourism. Behaviourists believe that attitudes and responses are the result of 'conditioning' or education. The classic example of behaviourist conditioning is the case of Pavolv's dogs. These animals were consistently fed when a bell was rung and thus came to associate food with the sound of a bell, eventually coming to salivate whenever a bell rang whether or not food appeared. Of course, it is true that we *learn* to behave in certain ways, but behaviourists miss out the vital element of self-consciousness, reflective and reasoning power *and* emotional response. All these are features of specifically human development and psychology, and they more plausibly account for the variable element in human behaviour and our reactions to the environment.

To 'condition' human beings is no simple process; they do not respond with the same predictability as Pavlov's dogs. Nevertheless, behaviourist arguments are popular and seem, to some, to accord with 'common sense'. People believe, for example, that children who watch violence on television will become violent, although evidence to support this view is confused; others argue that men who have witnessed violent behaviour by their fathers will grow up to be violent, or that men who consume pornography will act out its fantasies in real life. In fact, human psychology is much more complicated than that, but explanations of this kind are comforting precisely because they avoid the complex and difficult roots of human behaviour. Some feminists, therefore, argued that male violence, especially the sexual violence with which they were particularly concerned, was the result of direct example; it was a simple and plausible explanation. It could also seem progressive and optimistic. Behaviourist theories do not involve belief in an unchanging human nature; on the contrary, the human infant is an 'empty page' on which any 'programme' can be written.

Yet this theoretical cocktail of biologism and behaviourism is lethal. To see men as naturally programmed for violence is to endorse the most conservative views on human nature, to see it as unchanging and essentially unchangeable. Hence it would presumably be of little use to attempt to alter attitudes and the social climate, futile to argue that men should share equally in housework and childcare responsibilities if, at the same time, you saw them as so programmed – whether by their hormones or by conditioning – that they could not change at all. Also, to argue that men *are* programmed in this way is to absolve them of responsibility for their behaviour. At the same time, it is illogical then to yoke this view in with a belief that men are 'conditioned' to violence in a straightforward way, that if you simply took the toys from the boys you would destroy their fantasies and their aggression in one clean gesture.

The alternative view was that women and men are 'socially constructed' in complex ways to behave as we do. We internalize ideals of femininity and masculinity in part because of the influence of our parents upon us and our deep relationships with them. It is not an intellectual process of education or copying but an intense dynamic of family and social interaction that produces both conformity and resistance to oppressive norms of behaviour.

To combat this system of oppression was a daunting task, and it is perhaps not surprising that in the 1980s the impetus of campaigning feminism began to weaken. There has been piecemeal change. Feminist ideas have percolated into public awareness, although often in a distorted form. Some professional women have made some advances, although on the other hand there are now many more women in poverty. Feminists have had some success in creating a climate of opinion which has led to changes in police procedures in the investigation of rape and domestic violence; in England and Scotland there have been succesful prosecutions against men for rape in marriage. Yet the impetus of the law makers is much more towards protecting women as victims than towards empowering us as independent beings. Moreover, while women have become more visible in the workplace and in the street, the proliferating media and communications-dominated culture has not ceased to disseminate stereotypical images of women as sex objects, even if some alternative representations have also appeared. The culture and assumptions of advertising, the tabloids press, pop music, television and mass-market films have changed less than women's lives. Also, because the whole culture and communications industry has expanded, it may be that today we experience the sexual stereotyping of the mass media as having worsened, even if it also contains more 'alternative' or 'positive' images of women. Given that many more women now work in the media industries, it should be no surprise that there is continuing and widening feminist concern at the representation of women in the media.

It does, nevertheless, seem extraordinary that at the present time the campaigns against pornography are virtually the only visible, activist feminist campaigns. While rape crisis centres, the National Abortion Campaign and women's refuges struggle for lack of funds, anti-pornography campaigns have achieved a high profile and much feminist – and non-feminist – support. We believe that this is a sign not of the strength of the women's movement today but of its weakness.

Today, the group of feminists who campaign against pornography appear not to question the illogicalities upon which their campaign rests. For them, men and women are fundamentally and totally different and, according to their theory, all men are potential rapists waiting to be activated by pornography. At the same time, the emphasis on equally oppressive but non-sexually explicit representations of women in the media has fallen away. Feminists who campaign against pornography devote little attention to any of the many other images which reinforce women's traditional roles. In fact, the anti-pornography campaign is concerned entirely with the depiction of *sex*. The belief that there is a direct link between one particular kind of media representation – pornography – and the level of violence towards women in society, has obliterated analyses of other sources of female oppression. Now the sole concern is images whose purpose is to arouse sexual feeling. The alarming and paradoxical result of this is that we have heard more and more about one particular source of sexist imagery and less and less about the other campaigns that once seemed so important, as increasingly pornography has come to seem to be the central issue for feminists – so much so that today it is widely believed that all feminists are opposed to all pornography. Worse, it coincides with the concerns of the moral right and the law and order lobby, who wish to delegitimate and if possible censor all views which do not accord with their own.

What a contrast between today's campaigns against pornography and the many-sided activism of the seventies. Then, the aim was to build women's confidence, to increase our independence and autonomy, to transform society. This was a challenge to traditional, patriarchal right-wing morality, not a capitulation to it. Today, by contrast, the anti-pornography campaigns rely on the idea of women as victims; not much confidence-building there. They offer no new ideas, since, whatever they allege to the contrary, their view of pornography is identical to that of traditional conservatism. They offer no remedies save more censorship at the margins of the mass media, leaving untouched and uncriticized the much more pervasive daily diet of sexist, but not explicitly sexual, images. All that the campaign has achieved is to give undeserved respectability to the beliefs of the moral right and the fundamentalist lobby. It has worsened divisions amongst feminists and given the public the idea that all feminists are of their view. One result of this last is that it has damagingly taken over the Labour Party, becoming part of its new Kinnock-led 'respectability'.

Could it be that, like so many others, the anti-pornography campaigners have fallen for the view that, because we live in a 'media society', the media is the only reality?

4. Feminism and Cultural Politics

As we have already seen, criticism of images of women, particularly in the mass media, has been part of feminist thought since the modern women's movement took shape. In western European and American culture, the stereotyped image of women is far from flattering or truthful. With a few exceptions, media portrayals of women are still patronizing and sexist: women are seen as bimbos without a brain in their pretty heads or as competent mums with no interests other than their demanding families; and in the most abusive examples, as creatures who secretly enjoy being beaten and raped, indeed ask for it with their appearance or behaviour. The most we are offered is the new stereotype of the 'superwoman', juggling children, job and lovelife.

Feminists have responded with books and articles addressing the problem of the portrayal of women in literature, film and advertising, for example: *Is This Your Life? Images of Women in the Media* (King & Stott (eds) Virago 1977). There has been a successful feminist analysis of the images from popular culture and advertising – and a lively critique. The collision of witty, angry women with offensive gender-stereotyped representations has provided some of the best known and remembered images of 'feminism' in western society. For example, the photographic books *Spray It Loud* (Routledge and Kegan Paul 1982) and *Louder Than Words* (Pandora Press 1986) by Jill Posener showed graffiti on advertising billboards making witty and to-the-point criticism of those advertisements. 'If this car was a woman, it would get its bottom pinched,' was defaced with the words, 'If this woman was a car she'd run you down.' Judith Williamson, in *Decoding Advertisements* (Calder 1978), also commented on modern advertising from a feminist perspective. Slowly, advertising companies began to take notice, although only within certain limits.

'The consumer is not a moron, she is your wife,' said David Ogilvy, the director of one of the world's largest advertising corporations, making a clumsy attempt to address the problem of negative stereotypes of women in adverts. Ogilvy made this observation in the 1970s. Unfortunately, although the influence of feminism on advertising has brought us images of men happily stuffing washing machines and Norma the insurance expert, not that much has changed. The beauty of Singapore's women, especially those who work as flight attendants, is still advanced as a reason to visit that country. The Oxo family daughter cooks to catch a man. And two little girls can still be shown engaged in very unpleasant rivalry in a detergent advert over whose pile of towels is fluffier.

Our objection to the campaigns against pornography

– that they place it at the centre and as the main or even sole cause of women's oppression – leads us to a much wider definition of cultural politics. We don't want the same oppressive culture without the pornography; we believe that feminists should be campaigning for different cultural practices across a wide spectrum. The sets of ideas that encourage men to believe that they have the right to dominate women in all areas of life, and specifically have rights to harass and molest us sexually, didn't initially come from pornography. It is the other way round; pornography can be used to express underlying beliefs about men's superiority and to testify to men's greater access to power. For example, a sizeable number of Church of England clergymen have violently opposed, and continue to oppose, the ordination of women on grounds that often appear extraordinarily insulting and sexist. The majority of these men, however, would also strenuously oppose the proliferation of pornography. It is not because they have seen pornographic material that they believe women to be inferior; their conviction of female inferiority arises from a particular interpretation of Christian beliefs and scriptures.

Feminist cultural politics is a critique of all cultural representations, not just, or most importantly, sexually explicit ones. One of the first books of the contemporary women's movement, Kate Millett's *Sexual Politics* (Sphere 1971) examined the portrayal of women in the work of three 'great' twentieth century authors: D.H. Lawrence, Henry Miller and Norman

Mailer. These men wrote about the sexual relations between men and women in ways that Kate Millett and many other women found deeply disturbing and problematic. Millett challenged the notion that their work ought to be considered high art and therefore beyond this sort of social and political criticism. She revealed the misogyny to be found in the portrayals of women characters as objects to be fucked, deceived and despised.

Feminist cultural criticism has a double purpose. The first is to deepen our understanding of the forms of sexism that surround us, which are so familiar that we often take them for granted. Janice Winship has shown how women's magazines not only portray stereotypes of women that feminists wish to reject, but also accomplish extraordinary ideological feats such as making the drudgery of cooking and cleaning romantic, by posing it as 'how to keep your man', and making romantic passion domestic, by having marriage as the only satisfactory resolution of the story, (see 'A Woman's World: Woman – an Ideology of Femininity' in *Women Take Issue*, Women's Studies Group, Centre for Contemporary Cultural Studies (eds), Hutchinson 1978). Seeing the way this is done in women's magazines attunes us to the way it is done in our own lives; the way we too often associate having children with womanly fulfilment or a perfect complexion with sexual attractiveness.

The second purpose is more directly related to cultural politics: it is to understand how the various media and genres *work* in producing meanings, with a view to sabotaging or displacing that work and to finding ways of producing new meanings. At first, these studies tended to concentrate, as Kate Millett did, on the ways in which male-authored texts presented images that were oppressive to women. The assumption was that women would inevitably be oppressed, as long as these were the only images available. As feminist studies developed, though, it became clear that women readers are not just the hapless victims of the novels, films and magazines they are exposed to. Even the simplest of genres have some complexity and some space for alternative readings. In the classic films of Katharine Hepburn there is an appealing and convincing presentation of an independent woman, and many of us remember this much more clearly than the endings where she charmingly knuckles under to Spencer Tracey. Even Doris Day is reluctant at first to settle down with the boy next door, so providing an image of resistance as well as the more obvious one of conformity. Films, books and pictures do not have a single meaning that is fixed and inherent. Although they may lead you in a certain direction, much depends upon the context and on what you want to get out of it.

Feminists, then, on the one hand attempted to critique and rework mainstream culture and institutions, including all the branches of 'serious' art, and also devoted prodigious energy to an alternative culture of their own. For example, heated debate took place over whether a theoretical essay written in 'non-sexist' language could be taken seriously as a piece of academic work. Should we stick to recognized mainstream forms of scholarship in order to ensure that our ideas were taken seriously? Or should we refuse to have any truck with the elitism and exclusiveness of academic forms, exploring instead an alternative women's language and aiming for an audience of other women rather than academic men?

But perhaps the most important target of feminist cultural criticism was popular culture, and it may have been the emphasis on popular culture that led the debate in the direction of pornography. Although the meanings of popular culture are complex, it is quite hard to break with the dominant, elitist view which perceives it as unworthy and inferior. Pornography was surely the most unworthy and 'low' of all. Moreover, it was a partly hidden manifestation of popular culture, for women at least. This made it seem very sinister to some feminists. They effectively sided with the dominant, male, elitist pundits of western 'high' culture in perceiving in pornography the lowest kind of popular culture. Popular culture has often been seen as a flood of propaganda, as rubbish undermining the nation and destroying initiative, character and morals. Hollywood, Westerns, romantic fiction, the popular press have all been attacked in this way. Andrea Dworkin's attack on pornography is within this well-established tradition.

We, in contrast, would reiterate the following.

FEMINISM AND CULTURAL POLITICS

Feminist criticism of images of women in literature and other cultural arenas has been immensely important. It has been central to revealing the oppressive nature of the domestic and sexual relations between the sexes and women's place in the wider world. The criticism of sexually explicit material, too, has highlighted acutely painful aspects of male-dominated sexuality. But the implications of this work for feminist politics are far from clear-cut. If feminists have been able to uncover new meanings in old art and literature – and in pornography – then misogynists may be able to ignore the author's intention in feminist work. Culture cannot be divided into feminist and anti-feminist, for it is always a question of how we engage with culture, and every engagement is a voyage of discovery.

5. Three Common Arguments Used in Defence of Censorship

Three arguments recur time and again in discussions about censorship and pornography. Feminists who would not support state suppression of any other form of speech are willing to suspend their principles when it comes to pornography. They most often give the following reasons: (1) 'Pornography is the theory, rape is the practice', meaning that rapists are inspired to act by the things they see in pornography; (2) 'Pornography is itself violence against women', meaning that the very process of making pornography always harms women and that images themselves may constitute acts of violence; and (3) 'Pornography is incitement to sexual hatred', which is essentially an argument that male desire, if activated by pornographic images, is not so much lust as misogyny. Sexual desire itself becomes tainted by its association with sexually explicit imagery. In fact, this is a weak version of the argument made by some feminists that *all* heterosexual sex, particularly penetration, is merely the eroticization of power. Thus desire for sex is equated with desire to harm.

THREE COMMON ARGUMENTS

1. 'PORNOGRAPHY IS THE THEORY, RAPE IS THE PRACTICE.'

One commonly rehearsed view is that consumption of pornography causes rape and other acts of violence against women. In fact, the evidence, although conflicting and thus rather confused, does not substantiate the claim. Evidence which is claimed to link pornography and violence is of three main types: anecdotal or 'hearsay' testimony; evidence from psychological experiments; and the analysis of the correlation between the statistics on the availability of pornography and the incidence of violent crimes against women.

There is anecdotal evidence on both sides of the argument. It is said, for example, that the 'Moors Murderers', Ian Brady and Myra Hindley, regularly 'used' pornographic magazines. However, no connection between the pornography and the crimes has ever been proven. At the most, then, this constitutes an 'association': Ian Brady read the works of the Marquis de Sade and Ian Brady committed the murders. This does not amount to proof of a causal link. Of course, if there *were* a direct correlation between use of pornography and the commission of violent sex crimes, then all the men who use pornography and those who create much of the material as well, would logically be found to commit many more crimes than they actually do. As it is, the evidence shows that sex offenders have been exposed to pornography *later* than other men and have seen *less* of it. At the same time there are men who have committed violent acts against women who have been pre-occupied by non-pornographic images in art and literature. One multiple child murderer, for example, was said to be haunted by the episode in the Old Testament in which Abraham is instructed by God to sacrifice his son, Isaac. Almost any stimulus *may* act as a trigger to sexual arousal or to violent impulses, or both.

Some anti-pornography feminists maintain that the most important anecdotal evidence comes from women who say that pornography played a role in causing them to be raped. In these cases women have testified that their assailants were known to use pornography or that pornography was present and used during assaults. Women who have been raped by their husbands or lovers sometimes feel that, if these men also read pornography, there is a relationship between their consumption of pornographic images and the abuse. However, this does not explain why the vast majority of men who read pornography do not rape, nor does it take into account the many violent husbands and lovers who physically, psychologically and sexually abuse their partners without reference to pornography. Perhaps most importantly, it ignores the many and varied other means society has used, to much better effect, in order to promote the view that males 'own' the domestic and sexual services of their female partners.

Some rapists have indeed been known to bring

themselves to arousal in the course of an assault by looking at pornography. What this tells us is that these men are *not* motivated to rape because they have already been aroused by pornographic images, but rather that they have already decided to rape without being aroused, and need some way to arouse themselves in order that they may rape. It says nothing, however, about whether they would have assaulted women if there were no pornography available; they might simply have used other, perhaps more horrible, means to bring themselves to erection.

The evidence from psychological experiments is conflicting and unsatisfactory. One type of experiment uses reports of both male and female 'subjects', who are said to feel more aggressive after seeing films of sadomasochistic sex and gang rape than after watching 'non-aggressive' sex. This may support one aspect of the anti-pornography case, but it contradicts other elements of it; the essentialist argument often put forward as a reason why women need to be protected from 'naturally' violent men is that women are *not* sexually aggressive.

This kind of research must be treated with caution. Reporting by experimental subjects may be inaccurate. The subjects may 'report' what they think the experimenter wants to hear; they may be influenced by the views of other 'subjects'. (This phenomenon is illustrated by the famous psychological experiments in which subjects were asked to compare the lengths of lines displayed to them. In one experiment, if the first three or four 'subjects' claimed that the shorter line was longer, then other subjects would make similar fallacious claims). Similarly, anti-pornography campaigners are fond of citing as evidence the fact that sex offenders sometimes claim that they committed their crimes because they used pornography, i.e. that it was the pornography that gave them the bad ideas. But anyone can see why such testimony must be viewed with scepticism. In the first place, it is a way whereby the offender may shift the blame or relieve himself of some of the guilt; it may also be the result of treatment programmes run by counsellors who themselves believe that pornography is at the root of sexual violence, and who therefore, without necessarily consciously intending to, influence the offenders in this direction.

Secondly, there are significant variables which the aggression studies do not take into account. For example, it has been shown that women are sexually aroused by exposure to pornography, although they report that they are not; what could this mean to our assumption's about *men's* reactions to pornography? Do the psychologists consider the effect on arousal from exposure to non-pornographic violent films such as Martin Scorsese's *Mean Streets*, which contains many extremely violent images? In addition, the material used in experiments about pornography which is said to be violent, must either be constructed in the laboratory, which calls into question just what application these studies have to real life, or must be subject to the same restrictions that limit what is available in the market place.

And thirdly, of course, the studies themselves are performed in the artificial environment of the laboratory, and can tell us very little about how people actually use pornography and behave in other environments as a result. Whatever these studies may reveal about male sexual arousal, it does not follow that these very same men are likely to commit rape after exposure to violent pornography. The opposite argument is sometimes made, in fact: that pornography offers a form of release to those who might *otherwise* commit acts of violence.

As for statistical data, evidence of this sort must be carefully examined before any conclusions are drawn. For example, between 1972 and 1979, there was an increase in the UK in the amount of British pornography with explicit sexual content. The number of reported rapes also increased during those years. But, in the same period, there was a reduction in the amount of *hard core* pornography, and an increase in all violent indictable offences. So no clear conclusions can be drawn here about any causal connection between pornography and rape. Finally, the legislation of pornography in Sweden, Denmark, West Germany and Holland has not increased the sex crime figures in those countries. (For further discussion of the history of experiments on the subjects of pornography and violence, see *Pornography: Impacts and Influences: A Review of Available Research*

Evidence on the Effects of Pornography by Dennis Howitt and Guy Cumberbatch (HMSO 1990).)

Pornography is often criticized for 'objectifying' women. It is not always clear what is meant by this, but part of what is meant is the treatment of women as means to ends. The man who reads his copy of *Penthouse*, holding it with one hand, can treat the women depicted on its pages as wanting whatever he wants them to want. But objectification of this type may not always be sexist or demeaning to women. 'Objectification' occurs in the fantasies of many lovers of both sexes who treat one another as autonomous and equal.

The much quoted slogan, 'Pornography is the theory, rape is the practice,' suggests a simplistic model of human behaviour. People are seen as robots, switched on or off by a pornographic image. Real people, women and men, react in much more complicated ways to stimuli that surround them.

2. 'PORNOGRAPHY IS VIOLENCE AGAINST WOMEN.'

Many feminist critics of pornography argue that pornography is itself a form of violence. Andrea Dworkin, for example, has described what she views as particularly nasty pornography: snuff movies and magazines in which women are chained and tied.

There is no evidence that 'snuff' movies (in which an actual murder is supposed to be seen on screen) have ever existed. If they do exist, then of course the perpetrators are real murderers and should be treated as such, and subject to prosecution. In her book *Hard Core* (Pandora 1990), however, the film critic Linda Williams investigated the case of the film *Snuff*, which was released in the United States in 1976. She states that, 'the film in question, although unquestionably violent and especially, if not exclusively, so towards women, does not belong to the pornographic genre, unless the fantastic special effects of exploitation horror films are included in its definition.' She goes on to explain what happens in the film: a progression from a 'slasher' sequence in which an actress appears to be stabbed, to a scene which is intended to seem real because the audience is encouraged to believe that it is snatching an unintended glimpse of a murder 'off-camera'. What Williams calls 'the signals of documentary evidence' are used; a character says on the soundtrack that the film has 'run out' before the 'murder', there are voices after the screen has gone black, there are no credits. In other words, it is made to appear like an amateur movie of a real event. In fact, as the *New York Times* said on 27 February 1976, 'Nobody actually gets killed.' The New York City District Attorney responded to the public outcry over the film by interviewing the actress who supposedly had been murdered in the film (*New York Times*, 10 March 1976). Nevertheless, the snuff movie has become an urban legend.

The most widely read heterosexual male pornographic magazines – *Penthouse, Playboy* and *Mayfair* – do not incorporate images that could be called violent. They contain pictures of women, either naked or clad in lingerie, and some of the costumes are fetishistic. Anti-pornography campaigners have argued that these costumes symbolize violence if, for example, a woman is wearing a chain, or leather. Many mainstream fashions, however, also fetishize parts of the body by exaggerating or emphasizing certain characteristics such as breasts or feet, and to say that such garments actually constitute violence is to treat symbolism as actual behaviour. These magazines also contain captions and stories that are blatantly sexist and demeaning to women; for example: 'Girls come in two types and sizes. There are the tall, cool and sophisticated ones, and the small, cute, bouncy ones. If your favourite is the latter you'll love Zoe' (*Mayfair*). They do not portray violence in any obvious sense and, since sexist as opposed to sexually explicit material is widespread throughout society, it seems arbitrary to target only the latter.

In addition to pornography designed for hetero-sexual men there is pornography for gay men and we have now seen the beginnings of pornography for heterosexual and lesbian women. Some feminists argue that romantic fiction such as Mills and Boon is also a form of pornography for women, in that it purveys fantasies and has the potential to arouse. Some women, both heterosexual and lesbian, are also turned on by *Penthouse* images. Since there is very little in the way of sexual imagery specifically designed for women, it is difficult to know what turns women on. *The Kinsey Report* popularized the view that women respond less to visual imagery than men, but this finding has been questioned and may simply have been due to the fact that in the 1940s, when the original material for the report was gathered, the majority of women had no opportunity to discover whether they were turned on by pornography or not. Certainly, later studies have shown that heterosexual women do value some physical traits in men, although previous (male) researchers overlooked this because they had made false assumptions about what physical features women are influenced by.

It is important to remember that almost all pornographic material is representational. Images are not the same as what they depict. Even the minority types of pornography – for example, some hard core material which combines depictions of sexual activity with depictions of violence – cannot itself be on a par with real violence: warfare, rape, or natural disasters. Furthermore, the suggestion, made by some feminists, that much of the behaviour of men towards women can be described as violent, erroneously extends and waters down the sense of this term. It then begins to seem as if we are justified in objecting to men's behaviour *only* if it is 'violent'. This misses the reality, and one of the major difficulties of male/female relations, that sexism may not be violent at all and that many men may genuinely feel that wheedling, cajoling, whistling and certain kinds of remarks display not hostility but liking and desire for women.

Even if it were true that most pornography depicted violent activities, it would not follow that we should not be exposed to it. Ignorance can never make us safer. We would not want the media to ignore wars or violent crimes, simply because we might find the images distasteful. In fact, the opposite is more often the case; one complaint about the reporting and censorship of the media at the time of the Gulf War was that the war was sanitized by censorship and therefore made more palatable to the public.

The argument that the making of pornography itself constitutes violence against women is fuelled by a belief, common among anti-pornography campaigners, that women do not really like sex. The popular stereotype in which women, who are not really interested in sex, perform sex only under pressure from men, forms the foundation of a theory that every women who appears in visual pornography must have been forced to perform the acts shown, as no woman would actually wish to do these things. This assumption is applied to the full range of sexual activities, including and, in some cases, especially, to common sexual intercourse. Some feminists say that, therefore, to portray women as enjoying these acts constitutes a misrepresentation of women. But the facts do not support this portrayal of women; in reality, many of us enjoy penetrative sex with men as well as lesbian sex or other sexual practises.

There is the added complication that images such as

those of women being tied up or spanked appeal to both male and female sadomasochists, who enjoy this kind of theatrical play in their sexual fantasies. These sorts of images have also been called 'violence' but these fantasies and practices are entered into consensually and are enjoyed by both partners; a far cry from real sexual assault. All evidence shows that a sexual preference for dominance or submission is by no means an indicator of personality or behaviour toward others. It is well known, for example, that some men who enjoy masochistic and submissive sexual activities are assertive and dominant socially and often hold responsible and powerful jobs such as judges, MPs and lawyers. Much the same is true for women. Sexual fantasies and sexual behaviour do not necessarily mirror attitudes and behaviour outside the context of sexual activity.

Many other images – the housewife on her knees scrubbing the floor, or the secretary making tea for the boss – are as degrading to women as pornographic pictures. The 'Page Three' model is presented to readers as glamorous, young and above all successful and well paid. This too may well be a fantasy but, although it is degrading to represent women as nothing but a pair of boobs, pornographic images rarely portray them as nothing but this, while the traditional image of the housewife is, in fact, much more likely to be taken as signifying an all-embracing role.

3. 'PORNOGRAPHY IS INCITEMENT TO SEXUAL HATRED.'

Feminists in the UK who advocate the use of the law in relation to pornography strongly deny that they are pro-censorship. Legislation, they assert, would be based on civil rights: women's civil rights. Feminist members of the Campaign Against Pornography (CAP) and the Campaign Against Pornography and Censorship (CPC) refer to the ordinance drafted for the City of Minneapolis by Andrea Dworkin and Catherine MacKinnon, who, like the British campaigners, believe that pornography itself harms women and that it is a central element in maintaining male dominance. They have argued that pornography is a form of sexual discrimination because it is a specific harm that affects all areas of women's lives. In this booklet we have argued against these claims.

The Minneapolis Ordinance presents a long definition of pornography which includes the clause: 'Women are presented dehumanized as sexual objects, things or commodities ...'; implying that to be a sexual object is always and necessarily to be dehumanized. The Ordinance empowers individuals or groups of women to sue the producers and distributors of pornography for damages in civil court.

CPC advocates enacting similar legislation in the UK. Such legislation, they argue, would not be censorship; rather, it would be enabling, empowering women and making it possible for women such as

Linda 'Lovelace' Marchiano, who believe that they have been degraded or harmed by pornography, to take action against pornographers. (In her book *Ordeal*, Linda Marchiano alleges that she was coerced into making *Deep Throat*, and she argues that she was presented as a 'sex object' in the film, although she was the protagonist seeking gratification. Catherine MacKinnon used her case in a brief for the City of Indianapolis as an example of the kind of material that could be covered by law.) Using such legislation, according to CPC, a woman who has been assaulted could also take producers of a particular pornographic magazine to court if she can show that the man who assaulted her was inspired by that magazine. But this is only the illusion of protection; in fact it requires the woman to make an alliance with her rapist so that he could testify as to what magazine he used and that it was 'causal' to the rape. Moreover, such suits would be costly and the verdicts far from likely to support the woman's claims.

The CPC further claims that their proposed legislation is no different in form from legislation against incitement to racial hatred. They advocate introducing legislation for incitement to sexual hatred that directly parallels that for racial hatred.

There are, however, difficulties with the proposed legislation. First of all, let us look at the purported parallels with the race relations legislation. The race relations laws attempt to make incitement to racial hatred illegal. The Race Relations Act of 1976 and the

Public Order Act of 1986 contain clauses outlawing such actions. In assessing the effectiveness of any legislation to serve anti-racist, anti-sexist ends, we have to consider the political climate of the day. In the political climate of the 1980s and 1990s, attacks against minority groups – lesbians and gay men under Section 28 of the Local Government Act; 'immigrants' under the latest Immigration Act; other 'deviants' under any legislation that can be made to fit (for example, the prosecution of male homosexuals for gross bodily harm after participation in consensual sexual activity) – have been rife. However, since 1979, when the first Thatcher government came to power, there have been no major prosecutions under the 'incitement to racial hatred' clauses of the Race Relations and Public Order Acts. After the murder of a black man, Kingsley Reid was able to say publicly, 'One down, one million to go,' and not face charges. On the other hand, the Dowager Lady Birdwood, is being prosecuted for distributing anti-semitic literature and she has told the press she welcomes the hearing in court as another public forum for her views. This legislation is not working.

Moreover, there are significant and important differences between the Race Relations legislation and the proposed legislation about 'sexual hatred'. If the context made it clear that a reference to 'niggers, wogs and coons' stirred up racial hatred, then the connection between the racist language and the racist behaviour would be clear and overt. For a true parallel, 'incitement to sexual hatred' legislation would have to be used against men who called women things like 'birds, cunts and chicks' in public places, and meant these as terms of opprobrium. However, feminist campaigners are not proposing to bring actions in obvious cases like these; rather, they want pornography to be actionable and, as we have seen, the connection between pornography and 'incitement to sexual hatred' is not clear at all. In other words, it is those who produce certain images, not those who commit sexist or violent acts, who would be liable to prosecution in the proposed legislation.

Furthermore, those who publish race-hate material would, for the most part, say that they hate, mistrust and wish harm to those they are describing. Most sexist men, on the other hand, would generally claim to love women. More importantly, there is no evidence that a desire to engage in sexual acts with women corresponds to a desire to do them harm.

There are other difficulties with CPC's proposals. Any definition, if it is to incorporate the material its advocates want to see included, is likely to be broad and to encompass a whole range of sexually explicit materials. The definition provided in the Minneapolis Ordinance, using phrases such as 'the sexually explicit subordination of women' and 'postures of sexual submission', is both vague and all inclusive. Does the 'missionary position' automatically represent submission? If we read Andrea Dworkin's writings, and her general descriptions of heterosexuality as inherently and necessarily violent and unequal and oppressive to women, then it would come as no surprise to us to find that her intended target may actually have been *any* depiction of heterosexual sex. But even if this were not the case, leaving the average civil court judge who hears the case to interpret the meaning of the phrases is to open a Pandora's box of possible non-feminist readings of the law. (Dworkin and MacKinnon, in fact, were criticized in the US for relying on far-right moralists for support in New York State, where legislation using the language of their ordinance was proposed by a male, Catholic, conservative politician to combat sexually explicit material. The majority of feminists did *not* support them. It should not be lost on us that this legislation was very popular with right-wing legislators in Indianapolis and New York, nor that during the Meese Commission hearings on this issue, the feminist phrase 'degrading to women' was continually converted to 'degrading to femininity' by the men who ran the hearings.)

In any case, many feminist debates about sexuality, such as discussions about sadomasochism, were censored in Minneapolis since the court's briefs treated any such displays as depicting violence and aggression and not consensual sex, even if the practitioner had given evidence to the contrary. Here in Britain, even without legislation which specifically suppresses many 'unacceptable' forms of sexuality, both the Operation Spanner trial, where men were given prison sentences for participating in consensual SM sex, and the unsuccessful prosecution of a bookshop for selling a magazine about piercing, have shown that a similar closing of lines of debate could easily happen in this country. Already, the Obscene Publications Act and the Customs Act influence the stocking policies of small bookshops and the editorial policies of small magazines through fear of expensive prosecutions.

Finally, there are important differences between the United Kingdom and the United States which must be borne in mind in any discussion of the use of legislation. The USA has a Bill of Rights which sets out to protect certain individual freedoms. For example, the First Amendment to the United States Constitution guarantees freedom of speech. Any proposed local ordinances, as was the case in Minneapolis and Indianapolis, are subject to being overridden by the Constitution. Yet even the First Amendment's guarantee of free expression has been ignored from time to time in order to censor sexually explicit material, and obscenity laws have always been used to excuse political censorship; feminist works have been banned from public sale under obscenity laws, for example. Constitutional law ultimately defeats such legislation, as it did the Minneapolis and Indianapolis Ordinances, but only after lengthy and expensive court battles. The Bill of Rights may often be forgotten when it comes to the rights of women, black people and other marginalized groups, but it is an advance over Britain, which has no such thing, nor any freedom of information legislation. By law we have no rights at all in Britain and it is foolish to grant the authorities even greater power to restrict what we may say, publish, or see.

At present, we already have a great deal of censorious legislation which can be used by the courts as they think fit, in accordance with the dominant political climate. Compared with other western countries, Britain has very little variety in available sexual materials, thanks to the Obscene Publications Acts, the prudery of the Customs service and the timid stocking policies of most newsagents. It is this very censorship which is most responsible for the unbalanced and unrepresentative nature of pornography that feminists so often complain of: pictures only of women because the law makes us far too coy about portraying men; a lack of mutuality because the major news chains refuse sex magazines where pictures show people together; no significant visual narrative showing relationships because pornographic video is illegal. Well-intentioned people, such as the Education Officers in Dudley Council, who recently banned Postman Pat and Thomas the Tank Engine from nursery schools on the grounds that they are sexist, are only contributing to the repressive climate.

Despite their claims that they are not advocating censorship, this is effectively what anti-pornography feminists will achieve. Instead, feminists should be campaigning against restrictive laws and for the extension of civil rights.

6. Conclusion

Andrea Dworkin is wrong. It is not pornography itself that lies at the heart of women's oppression or indeed anyone's oppression. She has the problem turned upside down. Pornography may mirror the sexism of society but did not create it. Pornography as we know it – mass produced, for a mass audience, using primarily photograph, film and video – is a recent invention. Women's oppression, unfortunately, came long before porn.

We, Feminists Against Censorship, are highly critical of the current campaigns against censorship for the reasons we have indicated: the campaigns misunderstand the causes and origins of women's oppression and are likely to be ineffective in their own terms; that is, it is most unlikely that the incidence of rape and violence towards women and children will decline if pornography is banned. Historical evidence and evidence both from other industrial societies such as the USSR, and from developing countries, suggests that rape and sexual violence are unfortunately common rather than exceptional, and are certainly not dependent upon the existence of pornography. Furthermore, material likely to be banned under any new legislation will probably not be the material that the campaigners against pornography themselves believe to be the most harmful. Alternative feminist and gay publications are likely to be a prime target, and indeed, they already are.

A further point to be made is that censorship simply does not work. Anti-pornography campaigners would do well to take heed of the experience of Eastern Europe, where years of censorship have failed to diminish either the demand for pornography, now a flourishing industry there, nor for that matter anti-semitism, xenophobic nationalism and a host of other poisonous views. When censorship was lifted in post-Franco Spain, pornography flourished there as well. So we must regard with some scepticism the effectiveness of censorship as a strategy for social change.

Censorship in one area cannot be separated off from censorship in another area. A free and democratic society is one in which a diversity of views and behaviour is tolerated. That is not to say that there should or could be *no* restrictions on behaviour, or *no* regulation of what may be said, written or shown. We must recognize, however, that in a complex society, there is a wide range of views on matters to do with politics, sexuality and many other issues. Those who wield power can easily succumb to the view that they know best what is good for other people (people with less power normally) and seek to impose their views by preventing others from making up their own minds about allegedly 'seditious' or 'titillating' material, or material which will, in the minds of the legislators, 'undermine national character' or attack established religious beliefs. Scientists, secularists and many others have had to battle against the censors throughout the ages. Vested interests and established authorities always seem to want to keep the rest of us in ignorance. Whatever anyone's views about pornography in particular, the general approach should be that individuals may normally be trusted to make up their own minds. That, unfortunately, is not the view taken by current campaigns against pornography, nor, it would seem, by the Labour Party, which appears to be wholeheartedly behind Dawn Primarolo's Location of Pornographic Materials Bill. Leaving aside for now the question of whether it is desirable to set up separate licensed premises for sexually explicit material in the first place, let us consider the way material to be controlled is defined in the bill. Terms such as 'sexually humiliating or degrading' are subjective indeed. Who is to define what is 'sexually degrading'? Unelected trading standards officers? Local councillors? No matter how confident feminists may be that they know what they mean, there are those who consider any depiction of women as sexual beings, especially women enjoying being sexual, as degrading; any depiction of homosexuality as degrading; any depiction of women participating in sexual acts as necessarily objectifying them.

The setting up of licensed premises to sell only pornography is, in any case, censorship of a sort and, furthermore, it is open to all sorts of abuses and restrictions that those who claim to support the availability of some sort of sexually explicit material would do well to look out for. Initially the Primarolo Bill contained a fairly narrow definition of the material to be restricted. The stipulation was added that it would apply to material depicting men as well, therefore including homosexual material which only a few people argue has anything at all to do with the oppression of women. Most arguments against homosexual material come from those who disapprove of homosexuality anyway. There is now only one licensed gay sex shop in all of Britain. In the present political climate, how many local authorities will be willing to grant any more gay sex shop licenses?

The fact that pornography deals with sex makes it an attractive issue to those who campaign against it. It is a 'gut' issue. In our society we believe that sex is a very private and personal matter and, women at least, are often not accustomed to seeing pictures of sexual activity and the display of genitals. Images of attractive young women looking 'sexy' may arouse our own confusion or negative feelings about our own less-than-perfect bodies. Pornography may include images of sexual activities we believe to be bad, or somehow dirty, or coercive or violent, but it is important to remember that men and women may participate willingly in, for example, sadomasochistic activities.

The issue of those who participate in the *making* of

pornography is a separate one. Feminists Against Censorship opposes all coercion of sex workers, but again it is important to remember that pornography consists of images and that they are not just filmed or photographed acts of violence. Acts of violence committed in the course of making pornography are themselves illegal, and we in no way campaign to have rape, murder or torture made legal. Some of those who campaign for censorship have accused us of just this, but they are mistaken. We do not support sexism, racism or violence. We have simply had the gall, from their point of view, to disagree with the analysis and strategy of anti-pornographers.

We believe that feminism is about *choice*, about taking control of our lives and our bodies, and this must include our sexual choices. Much of the feminist criticism of both high street (so called 'soft') porn, and of alternative images, such as Della Grace's photographs of S/M lesbians, denies any possibility of consent or choice on the part of the women involved. From their point of view, all women are victims – except for the campaigners who are out to 'save' them.

Yet, after all, lesbians might find images of heterosexual sex unpleasant (they might, for that matter, be upset by all the heterosexual romance on TV and in films), while those who are not interested in S/M sex might feel uncomfortable looking at images to which they bring no prior experience and with which they therefore can't empathize, but this doesn't necessarily make any of these images inherently malignant or harmful. If everyone had the right to ban all images and written material which happened to offend them, how much would actually be left? If we were all only allowed to see and read that which offended no-one, culture would be utterly insipid – or more likely non-existent!

The distinction between 'erotica' and 'pornography', which the anti-pornographers have taken over from a mainstream elitist debate about what is artistically justifiable, tries to draw a clear dividing line between 'good' sex and 'bad' sex. We are not saying that all sex is automatically 'good' or that pornography can never be horrible or violent; we do feel that responses to explicit material are very subjective and that 'erotica' is what 'we' like while pornography is what 'they' like. Yet sometimes it is the 'pornography' that is the most interesting, creative and exciting; which, after all, is the purpose of the sexually explicit.

Western society over-values stereotyped ideals of sexual attractiveness and emphasizes the importance of sex in what are often unhelpful and disempowering ways. One result of this is that our insecurities about sexuality can be confusing and threatening. In a society in which sex is both a dirty joke and the most important thing about us, the key to happiness and a dark secret, it is much easier to criticize sexual images produced by other people than it is to examine our own fantasies and desires and take the risk of producing and being turned on by the representation of those desires and fantasies in words and pictures. It is easier to claim that women's sexuality is so colonized and so threatened that we can't possibly afford to do anything except batten down the hatches and try to get rid of everything we find unpleasant and nasty. It's much easier to assume that women who work in the sex trade must be abused victims, than to accept that their work can in some circumstances be their choice, and support them in their calls for better working conditions and less oppressive legal interference in their lives.

The campaigns against pornography are losing the feminist impetus that they started out with as they reach a wider audience and gain support from the moral right. The campaign is no longer primarily a critique of sexism, masculine power or patriarchal society. First it becomes a critique of the pornography industry: a 'billion dollar industry', as we're often told. Well, the food and garment industries are 'billion dollar industries' too, so what's new? If some people feel that it's wrong to profit from the sale of sexual imagery, why don't they campaign against those who make vast profits out of feeding us, often with polluted and dangerous food? To point the finger at the industry is to ignore the more important critique of sexism and of male power, which is what feminists should target. Of course, when the campaign then gets taken up by the 'moral majority', the target of their attack becomes the 'permissive society'; they want to *restore* patriarchal power, which they feel has been eroded by the greater freedom of choice, limited though it still is, that women have gained over the past thirty years.

We have seen the ways in which feminism has made a difference in the world. Women are taking control of their lives and at least some young women have more choices, including sexual choices, than they once did. We must defend those gains. We have a right to our own sexuality and many of us are taking the expression of our sexuality in public, in words and pictures, out of the hands of multinational corporations with their limited imaginations about what anyone does 'in bed'. Many women are taking risks to produce feminist sexual images, images which do not exploit either the viewer or the producer.

In the past decade, there has been an explosion of material produced by women, particularly by lesbians. In the United States, this began with the line drawings of the *Cunt Coloring Book* and there is now the explicit photography and stories of *On Our Backs* (the San Fransisco magazine). The lesbian film *Desert Hearts* has received fairly wide distribution, sex scene and all. In Britain, the lesbian erotic short story book *Serious Pleasure* is in two volumes (the Sheba Collective (eds) Sheba 1989 and 1990), and the sex magazine *Quim* has published two issues. Both the production and the consumption of pornography can be erotic acts, and we have the right to participate in these acts.

We must go on the offensive and stop being baited by those who call our defence of our sexual images oppressive, stop allowing them to set the agenda for what is and is not feminist. The battle against pornography, like the temperance movement at the turn of the century, is about much more than gin, videos, or 'vice'. To a disturbing extent, the present censorship campaigns could end up, as those former campaigns did, as one group of women attempting to control and regulate another, less privileged group. And all the while the real battle is elsewhere: it is the battle against public and private violence, against unequal pay structures, against a lack of opportunities for girls and women.

We support campaigns for greater freedom of expression in all forms of art and culture. We want better sex education. We want an end to the militaristic, imperialistic culture of our society, and an end to racist and sexist violence. These evils arise in part from poverty, exploitation and injustice, but also from the cult of the macho and the 'hard man'. Films and publications which glorify non-sexual violence probably do far more damage than 'Page Three' and *Hustler*.

It's time to name the real enemies.

Further Reading

Alison Assiter *Pornography, Feminism & the Individual* (Pluto 1989)

John Berger *Ways of Seeing* (Penguin 1972)

Rosemary Betterton (ed.) *Looking On: Images of Femininity in the Visual Arts and Media,* (Pandora 1987)

Varda Burstyn (ed.) *Women Against Censorship* (Vancouver & Toronto, Douglas & McIntyre 1985)

Angela Carter *The Sadeian Woman* (Virago 1982)

Gail Chester & Julienne Dickey (eds.) *Feminism and Censorship* (Prism 1988)

Beatrice Faust *Women, Sex and Pornography* (Penguin 1981)

Feminist Review (eds.) *Sexuality: A Reader* (Virago 1987)

FURTHER READING

Nancy Friday *My Secret Garden: Women's Sexual Fantasies* (Virago 1976)

Forbidden Flowers: More Women's Sexual Fantasies (New York: Pocket Books 1975)

Walter Kendrick *The Secret Museum: Pornography and Modern Culture* (Viking 1987)

Josephine King & Mary Stott (eds.) *Is this your Life? Images of Women in the Media* (Virago 1977)

Annette Kuhn *Cinema, Censorship and Sexuality, 1909-25* (Routledge 1988)

Kate Millett *Sexual Politics* (Sphere 1971)

Jill Posener *Spray It Loud* (Routledge & Kegan Paul 1982)

Jacqueline Rose *Sexuality in the Field of Vision* (Verso 1986)

Samois (eds.) *Coming to Power* (Samois 1981)

Lynne Segal *Is the Future Female? Troubled Thoughts on Contemporary Feminism* (Virago 1984)

Ann Snitow, Christine Stansell & Sharon Thompson (eds.) *Desire: The Politics of Sexuality* (Virago 1986)

PORNOGRAPHY AND FEMINISM

Mariana Valverde *Sex, Power and Pleasure* (Toronto: The Women's Press 1985)

Carole S. Vance (ed.) *Pleasure and Danger: Exploring Female Sexuality* (Routledge and Kegan Paul 1984)

Simon Watney *Policing Desire: Pornography, AIDS and the Media* (Methuen 1987)

Linda Williams *Hard Core: Power, Pleasure and 'The Frenzy of the Visible'* (Pandora 1990)

Elizabeth Wilson *What is to be Done about Violence Against Women?* (Penguin 1983)

Janice Winship 'A Woman's World: *Woman* – an Ideology of Femininity' in Women's Studies group, Birmingham centre for Contemporary Cultural Studies, (eds), *Women Take Issue: Aspects of Women's Subordination* (Hutchinson 1978)

CONCLUSION

FEMINISTS AGAINST CENSORSHIP
can be contacted at
38 MOUNT PLEASANT LONDON WC1X 0AP